# SECONDHAND WORMS

## BY

## HERBERT JAXON

GHP

Grosvenor House
Publishing Limited

This book is published by
Grosvenor House Publishing Ltd
Link House
140 The Broadway, Tolworth, Surrey, KT6 7HT.
www.grosvenorhousepublishing.co.uk

A CIP record for this book
is available from the British Library

ISBN 978-1-80381-970-9
eBook ISBN 978-1-80381-971-6

For Lucy, Amy, Max, Ronnie, Dan, and Oliver

## *WHAT THEY SAID ABOUT MR JAXON'S VERSE.......*

I think it's good. (*Mr Jaxon's old mum.*)

No. (*Response of Mr Jaxon's English teacher at school, when asked by a jaxonian classmate if he agreed that Mr Jaxon's verse might have some merit.*)

Everything you write is just another pathetic attempt to be funny. (*The same English teacher, offering Mr Jaxon constructive criticism.*)

This is pretty dreadful. (*A different English teacher at the same school, when reviewing something Mr Jaxon had written.*)

Nobody's going to read your book. (*Mr Jaxon's wife.*)

The poems you write that are meant to be serious are funnier than the ones when you're trying to be funny. (*An imaginary friend[1] of Mr Jaxon, offering her own brand of constructive literary criticism.*)

No one will have understood the joke in that poem – you're too clever by threequarters. (*The same perceptive literary critic.*)

I don't know – I didn't read Herbert's poem to the end. (*Another friend of Mr Jaxon, when asked by this perceptive literary critic whether he agreed that no one would understand the poet's attempt at humour at the end of the poem.*)

---

[1] The lady is real; it is their friendship that is imaginary.

I still think it's good. (*Mr Jaxon's old mum, on being informed that other assessments of the merit of Mr Jaxon's work were available.*)

What you write might quite possibly be called *vers d'occasion.*[2] (*A censorious friend of Mr Jaxon.*)

You should have called your book: *Burn Before Reading.* (*Mr Jaxon's wife.*)

---

[2] Translator's note: *Secondhand worms.*

# CONTENTS

# YULETIDE WORMS

# SLEEP

At Christmas time some people cruise
Around the shops, wear out their shoes,
And stand in queues, as debt accrues,
Then crumple in a heap;
While Boxing Day brings gastric blues,
Stale turkeys, tough as kangaroos,
And tempers fray when West Brom lose,
That's why I choose to sleep.

Some deck their homes with frills and bells,
With tinsel, streamers, carousels,
Then fill the air with whoops and yells,
That make the neighbours weep;
They roast their bowels with caustic brews,
Drink up the booze, then use the loos,
With nary a thought for someone who's
Just trying to get some sleep.

The office party brings excuse
To fix illicit rendezvous,
Tu-whit, tu-woos, then toodle-oos,
And guilty secrets keep;
Astuter folk eschew those dos
And opt instead to woo the muse –
But all I really want's a snooze,
For I was born to sleep.

So, just stay calm – there's no alarm;
Don't be afraid you'll come to harm
When, oozing lots of oily charm,
Between your sheets I creep;
Although it might be dead of night,
Do not take fright – I will not bite;
Now, Sweetie, please turn out the light:
My sole delight is sleep.

*December 2011*

# BLANCANIEVES

I tiptoed out on Christmas Eve, when all at home were sleeping,
On frosty paths, and under wintry cloud;
Though all the while my wretched mobile phone would not stop
      bleeping,
The beating of my heart was twice as loud.

The night was dark, and bitter cold, but I was swept along
By promise of a woman's lurid charms;
And though I knew that what I did tonight was surely wrong,
The lure was strong from Blancanieves' arms.

There was a humble dwelling buried deep within a wood,
A workman's shack to which she held a key,
Where Blancanieves summoned me to meet her, when she could,
For lovers' trysts she conjured up for me.

Her father owned a big estate, awash with game and pheasant,
So she was rich, and proud, with looks to kill;
And she would treat the toughest man as if he were a peasant,
Then kick him out when she had had her fill.

When Blancanieves cast her spell no flesh and blood could linger:
She knew that when she kissed you, you stayed kissed;
And I confess she had me wrapped around her little finger,
Which, when she snapped it, I could not resist.

She'd texted me the previous day to fix another session,
And I was keen to meet her as before;
I knew, of course, to exercise the maximum discretion,
So crept downstairs, and softly closed the door.

Not finding time to wonder who was sending me a text,
I hurried on to meet my arch-intriguer;
Though she was overblown, and overpriced, and oversexed,
And I was overweight, and overeager.

Yet when I reached the shanty where the woman used to wait,
It stood in darkness, with no welcoming light;
All cold and damp, no candle flame, no fire in the grate –
I wondered if I'd got the venue right.

But as I thought to turn around and hurry home in tears,
An unseen hand drew open the front door,
And Blancanieves pulled me in, and hugged away my fears:
The warmth of her embrace betokened more.

And so began a night of lust, a bout of rawest passion,
Clandestine kisses in abundant measure;
Some ninety minutes filled with bliss – a quite humungous ration;
(A win for Albion scarcely matched the pleasure.)

Throughout our romping Blancanieves uttered not a sound,
Yet, truth to tell, her silence barely mattered;
I couldn't see her clearly, for the darkness was profound,
But, home in bed by five, she'd left me shattered.

On Christmas morn, still half asleep, I checked my phone for tweeting,
And clocked the message from the previous night:
"I have a headache, Herbert dear, and cannot make our meeting…"
It made no sense… Could I have read it right?

The steamy memories of our frolics fast were falling flat;
I faced the awkward truth against my will:
If Naughty Blanc had stayed at home, then who the blank was that?
Ah… England is a land of mystery still!

*December 2018*

# THE MISER'S EXCUSE

The Reindeer has all year to play,
And only works on Christmas Day;
On all the rest he snorts cocaine,
While Santa shoots it in the vein.

And, while the reindeer's taking sniffs,
The elves are busy rolling spliffs,
To keep Old Santa flying high,
Or sell to any kids who'll buy.

I simply can't abide their presence,
So, son, this year there'll be no presents;
But please, don't make me feel a louse:
I can't let junkies in the house.

*December 2003*

# TRUE LOVE

Most respected Sir, or Madam, though you don't know me from
      Adam,
I am writing to request a place to stay;
For the tale that I am telling saw me kicked out of my dwelling,
So I'm hoping that you won't turn me away.
Though it couldn't get much dafter, what's recorded hereinafter
May provide a timely wakeup call for those
Who allow clearheaded thinking to be clouded by hard drinking,
Which has, sadly, been the source of all my woes.

There are those who may be wondering what absurd degree
      of blundering
Caused my rapid slide from honour to disgrace;
Making me the butt of laughter: forced to wear, forever after,
An inverted *Tesco* bag to hide my face.
If my veil is unappealing, what this gunnysack's concealing
Is some madness that can never be undone,
For when alcohol's your master it can turn into disaster
What you think is just a harmless bit of fun.

Unacceptable societally, yet it all began so quietly,
When some playmates called to take me for a jar;
I was unenthusiastic, but they teased me with sarcastic
Jibes and insults till I joined them at the bar.
We went down the *Frog & Nightgown*, and I wouldn't care to
      write down
Quite how many pints I hoovered up unplanned;
I lost count at six or seven, but at least ten or eleven,
And on leaving I could barely even stand.

P'rhaps it sounded too bathetic, but my mates weren't sympathetic
When I said I fancied toddling home to bed;
They just gave me some old toffee about taking me for coffee
To an 'all-night tattoo parlour' place instead.
When we got there it was grotty, and jam-packed with dirty totty,
So I sussed at once that something wasn't right,
For the joint was just a sleazy, seedy front for a speakeasy,
Where illegal drinking carried on all night.

Someone hit me with a stinger, a one-sixty proof rum slinger,
After which they just kept hitting me with more,
Till I'd drunk so many highballs they were running out my
            eyeballs,
And my head was banging like the dunny door.
When it grew a little quieter the establishment's proprietor
Drew the raffle, while I scarfed another brew;
Heaven knows what made him pick it, but I'd bought the
            winning ticket,
And he told me I could choose a free tattoo.

News to set alarm bells ringing... But by then I'd started singing,
And was deaf to any word of good advice;
So, instead of just declining, I could hear myself opining
That: "The Sistine Chapel ceiling might be nice..."
"*Nah* – you don't want *nuffink* prissy, what'll make you look a cissy,"
Rasped the cruel, sadistic monster who's our host;
"What you want's a declaration, what I'll scribe to your dictation,
"Telling all the world the one you love the most!"

With my senses badly jaded I was easily persuaded,
And agreed to take my prize that very day;
So I told the sepsis seller I'd selected: 'I love Stella',
And suggested he infect me right away.
"Where d'you want it?" he entreated, (his expletives I've
      deleted),
"On your bicep, on your forearm, or your chest?"
"No, let's go for something torrid! Come on! Scrawl it on my
      fore'ead!
"FOUR-INCH CAPITALS in purple would be best!"

Not requiring any stencil he took up the electric pencil,
Inking in the script without another word;
The effect was copacetic, and my liquor anaesthetic
Meant that not a single squeal of pain was heard.
Waking up the following morning I could sense some trouble
      dawning,
As my bags were packed and dumped out in the snow:
"Who's this *Stella*, heart's abhorrence?" barked my wife, who's
      christened Florence,
(But behind her back she's known as 'Fratton Flo').

If she'd only let me tell her that the brazen 'I LOVE STELLA',
Branded brash upon my brow, was incomplete;
But she jumped to the conclusion, that the thrust of my allusion
Was a strumpet who lives halfway up our street.
If she'd listened to my pleading… But she left me
      scratched and bleeding,
And then threw me out as if I were a dog;
Yet the words she found suspicious merely lauded the delicious
*Stella Artois* I'd be drinking in the *Frog.*

Which is why, this festive season, there's a *bona fide* reason
Why I need to bum a lunch on Christmas Day;
So if you could spare a plateful I would be forever grateful,
And remain, your humble servant, *Herbert J.*

*post scriptum*

There's a final thing, but only as I feel a trifle lonely,
So I hope you will excuse this brief PS:
If you know of any Stella who is looking for a fella,
I'd be grateful if you'd send me her address.

*December 2021*

# CHIPS[3]

By the First of last December – maybe even late November –
My beloved had already dressed the tree;
And, with presents all surrounding, she had set my heart
      a-pounding
When she told me that the big one was for me.

It was (more or less) an oblong, and (I'd say) about two-foot long,
By some twelve or fourteen inches deep, and wide,
Bearing all the Christmas trappings, tawdry bows and gaudy
      wrappings,
Yet not offering any clue of what's inside.

While I fretted every minute, wondering what the deuce was in it,
*Liebling* wouldn't speculate, to my dismay;
She just laughed at my reaction, but surmised my Granny Jaxon
Must have left it on our step the previous day.

Yet the subject needed broaching, for with Christmas slow
      approaching,
We were both convinced there must be something wrong,
For the box seemed to be squeaking, and was definitely leaking,
Causing staining on the carpet, and a pong.

Such malodorous viscosity merely fuelled my curiosity,
And propelled my torment into overdrive;
Yet, despite my agitation, I resisted all temptation
To unwrap it till December twenty-five.

---

[3] Please be assured that this is a work of fiction, and that no children or animals were discommoded during its excretion. That said, none of the activities mentioned herein should be attempted except by a suitably qualified person.

But then, first thing Christmas morning, with my slumber-mate
    still yawning,
I rushed down and split the parcel open wide
With a chopper…! (Which was crazy, for I narrowly missed the
    lazy,
Cutie, kitty cat, curled up asleep inside!)

Early doors I was elated, though the puss looked dehydrated,
Lying motionless, pretending to be dead;
But when violently shaken he showed signs he might awaken,
And he came to life as soon as he'd been fed.

Looking back, I was quite smitten by that tiny little kitten,
Looking forward to some wild, ailuric fun,
But incipient jubilation was soon tempered by frustration
When the Memsa'ib told me all she wanted done.

In a manner magisterial, she began, in tones ethereal,
Listing hoops through which a new cat owner jumps:
First she mentioned vaccination, to ward off worm infestation,
Measles, migraine, mad cow, monkeypox and mumps;

After which he would need *chipping*, just in case he might be
    kipping,
Locked inside a garage, hidden out of sight.
She said with a chip behind him we would still be able to find
    him…
(That's if I have understood the last bit right.)

Madam's checklist was extensive, and it sounded quite expensive,
Though she knows I'm one for keeping down the cost…
Surely if a cheaper option could be found, then its adoption
Might put *Lucky* on the road, with nothing lost.

Mulling over *Frau*'s suggestions, was I really wrong to question
Splurging mega moolah on a moggy's health?
*Ergo* my amelioration was: *postpone* his vaccination
*Sine die*, and insert the chip myself.

There is no time like the present, even if a task's unpleasant,
So I set to work to *chip* him straightaway,
Though it's true that I proceeded, rather vague on what was
        needed,
When I kicked the carnage off on Innocent's Day.

With the work barely in motion, *Lucky* caused a great
        commotion…
(*¡Qué putada!* Chipping's *not* for the faint-hearted!)
He lent *no* cooperation, but a bigger complication
Didn't hit me till the operation started.

I was utterly unable to duct tape him to the table,
As he struggled hard and, angry and perplexed,
Started scratching me and spitting, so I wouldn't mind admitting
He'd a good idea of what was coming next.

All at once his crazed bionics triggered zany histrionics,
And he jactitated like a bucking steed;
I was shocked, to put it mildly, seeing limbs all thrashing wildly,
Like a hyperactive octopus on speed.

With my right hand round his paws, and with my left to clamp his
        jaws, and
All my body weight to stop his withers slippin',
And my knee to pin his tail down, so his chitlins couldn't flail
        round,
I had no free hand to force the flippin' chip in.

So I yelled to her indoors, who – I believe – was scrubbing floors, to
Drop her mop and come and offer me assistance;
I was hoping reinforcement might be taken as endorsement
Of my firm resolve to snuff out his resistance.

"*What the Dickens are you doing?*" screams my angel, venom
        spewing,
Spitting razor blades, and sounding sorely pained;
And, my efforts notwithstanding, she showed no more understanding,
Even after I had carefully explained

That the art of chip insertion needed far too much coercion,
And I hadn't realised till much too late,
That the orifice I'd chosen probably called for something frozen,
Rather than a soggy fried one off my plate.

We had eaten a fish supper, washed down with a welcome cuppa,
And I'd thought my chips had had a funny taste;
Well, *of course*, she had to fetch up that I'd smothered them with
        ketchup,
But I didn't want those chips to go to waste….

With a bellow of frustration, she cuts short my explanation,
Telling me I'm talking total taradiddle,
Adding when she mentioned *chipping* she meant *micro*chips – not
        flipping
*Findus* French fries from a freezer, filched from *Lidl*!

She averred the chipping process would give *Lucky*'s finder
        access
To his owner's contact details and address,
And the chip could take more data if we wished to add it later…
Then she helped me clean up *Lucky*'s mucky mess.

So we had him chipped professionally, but I have to add, confessionally,

That there must be more to chips than meets the eye:

For I've clicked on *Lucky*'s entrails but I still can't read my emails

From his microchip, and no one's told me why.

The whole mystery's uncanny, and I tend to blame my Granny,

Yet it's all *my* fault, according to my wife,

Who told Granny in a letter I'd have coped with poultry better,

As a turkey's just for Christmas – not for life.

*December 2022*

# L'EMMERDEUSE

La vie est dure, Marie-Estelle,
Pour moi, ton serviteur fidèle,
Un ingénu chétif et frêle,
Maltraité par ce monde cruel.

J'adore ton corps de violoncelle,
Ton derrière exceptionnel,
Mais dois atténuer mon zèle,
Car je suis moche, mais tu es belle.

En travaillant avec ma pelle,
Ou me servant de ma truelle,
Et même en faisant la vaisselle,
Je pense à toi, chère Mad'moiselle…..

Si je pouvais piquer les ailes
À une jolie hirondelle,
Je volerais à travers l' ciel
Pour te souhaiter un bon Noël!

Mais ta réponse habituelle
À mes bons vœux traditionnels,
Reçue sitôt, par courriel,
Me dit d'*abi in malam rem*!

Toi, qui n'as pas de parallèle,
Ignores mes pleurs continuels;
La vie est dure, Marie-Estelle,
Pour ceux qui vivent dans ta poubelle.

*December 2017*

# TALKING TURKEY

It was fairly late December – Christmas Eve, if I remember –
When I went to fetch my fowl for Christmas Day;
But the man at *Turkey Gobbler* made me nearly throw a wobbler,
And cast all my Christmas plans in disarray.

Said he wasn't a defrauder, but he "must've lost" my order,
So, for me, he "couldn't do a bloomin' *fing*,
"'Cos," if he was not mistaken, all his "blinkin' birds were taken,"
And he "wouldn't get no more before the Spring!"

As I couldn't find my chitty he was showing me no pity,
Till I threatened to chastise him with my shoe;
Whereupon the shifty blighter, turning fifty shades politer,
Said he'd, "try and *fink* of *somefink*," he could do!

So he scratched his head and pondered, then went out the back
        and wandered,
And came back, and tapped his nose, and winked, and said:
"I remember now – I'm sorry – I've got one 'fell off a lorry',
"You can 'ave 'im if you like – but 'e ain't dead!"

"One that's still alive?" I stuttered. "Keep your 'air on, guv!" he
        spluttered,
"*Can'tya* see you're in a *rarver* tricky spot?
"Do you want this bird, or *doncha*? Will you take 'im now, or
        *woncha*?
"Like I *toldya*, 'e's the only one I've got!"

"But I want him oven-ready!" "Not a chance! 'E isn't dead – 'e
"Must've *layed* down when 'e saw the butcher's knife;
"'E's a very clever birdy, and from what I over'eard, 'e
"Sort of 'acted dead', and that's what saved 'is life!"

"But I want him plucked and gutted!" "There's no time for that,"
      he tutted,
"I'm about to shut the shop, and toodle-oo!
"You can 'ave 'im if you're willin' to cough up *anuvver* shillin',
"But I'll 'ave to leave the butchery to you!"

Well, I wasn't very happy. When the *Turkey Gobbler* chappy
Led the turkey in it gave me quite a peck;
But, since nothing else was proffered, I just took the bird he
      offered
And went home to wring the little rascal's neck.

When the time came to apprise him it was time to marmalise him,
I was quite prepared to listen to him squawk,
To remind me he objected, but the last thing I expected
Was to hear the turkey turn to me and *talk*!

"Do not slay me, gentle master; if you did 'twould spell disaster,
"For as far as I've been led to understand,
"Though you've paid an extra shilling, you and I could make a
      killing –
"I'm the most intelligent turkey in the land!"

"You can talk?" I interjected. "I can *speak*," the bird corrected,
"And my diction has impressed you, I can tell;
"But, while speech is entertaining, I'm a scientist by training –
"Though I speak ten other languages as well!

"I have mastered quantum physics, found a cure for
      pneumo-phthisics,
"And a way to change base metals into gold!
"I've corrected Einstein's theory, cleared the algae from Lake Erie,
"And my youth elixir stops you growing old!

"Stoichiometry is easy; rocket science, easy-*peasy*;
"And I've won three Nobel Prizes in a row!
"So if you should ever harm me folks are going to call you barmy!
"But perhaps you'd like a taste of what I know?

"Question me on any topic, for my brain's kaleidoscopic!
"Any subject – science, literature or art!
"Come along, just try and test me, but you'll never *ever* best me,
"For I've learnt all *Wikipaedia* by heart!"

So, "*OK*," I said, "*whatever*! Tell me now, if you're so clever,
"Which team won the Cup in nineteen fifty-four?
"And you're answer's not complete unless you know which side
        was beaten,
"And I also need to know the final score."

Without pause for contemplation – not a *moment's* hesitation! –
He responded with the air of one who knew,
That, in '54, at Wembley, the West Bromwich team's assembly
Had defeated Preston by 3 goals to 2!

He was right, which quite amazed me; his composure almost
        fazed me,
But I knew I mustn't crumple under stress;
Preston *and* West Brom in tandem? Had he picked them out at
        random?
Could his answer just have been a lucky guess?

I admitted he'd delayed me – one more answer might persuade me:
"Who wore number 4 for Albion in that game?"
But the turkey didn't buckle, as he told me with a chuckle:
"Jimmy Dugdale was the West Brom player's name!"

When I grabbed him by the wattle he was easy enough to throttle,
Though he swore a bit, and kicked, and effed, and clawed;
I don't want to sound malicious, but he tasted more delicious
Once I knew that I'd exposed him as a fraud.

Those who understand their soccer will have spotted why his
        shocker
Of an answer meant the bird could not survive:
Albion's number 4 was cuddly little Scotsman, Jimmy *Dudley*!
Jimmy *Dugdale*? He was wearing number *5*!

If that bird was half as clever as he claimed, then he would never
Have presumed to save his giblets from the stock;
There's a moral to this ditty: when you've gone and lost your
        chitty,
Never trust a cocky turkey talking cock.

*December 2015*

# BE CAREFUL WHAT
# YOU WISH FOR

I was unwrapping presents one chill Christmas morn,
Feeling festive, elated, and glad to be born,
When a curious parcel dropped out of the tree,
Smelling rather unpleasant and falling on me.

"Who on earth can have sent it," I pondered, perplexed;
The uxorial person said: "Open it next;
"It'll be from your granny," was what she opined,
As I chortled aloud! Was she out of her mind?

"A gift from *yer grannie*?" I giggled with glee,
"Tell me: why would that pigdog send presents to me?"
Then she rolled her eyes upward, while stifling a scream,
And contorting a pout that would curdle ice cream.

"I don't *mean* Grannie *******[4], you ignorant drone!
"It's from Old Granny *Jaxon*, that elderly crone
"Who resides in a cave in a cliff by the sea –
"You can bet it's from her if it's smelling of wee!"

And then, flouncing her tresses, she left in a huff,
Having sprouts to dismember and turkeys to stuff…..
All alone with my prezzie, I fervently tried
To conjecture what Granny had hidden inside.

It was too big for *Lego*, too lumpy for socks,
And without any ticking, so that ruled out clocks,
But I found when I shook it it gave off a slurp
That resembled my granddad's post-prandial burp,

---

[4] And here may be inserted the trochaic nickname of any family enemy.

Ergo possibly liquid, which broadened my grin,
As my thoughts turned to *Tizer*, or *Tanqueray* gin,
So removing the wrappings brought quite a surprise:
Just a rusty old oil-lamp, bedecked with dead flies.....

It was greasy, malodorous, covered in grime
And in cobwebs accrued over aeons of time,
And emitting the stench of a foul sewer pipe,
So I whipped out my hankie to give it a wipe.

My nose-rag was grotty, and snotty as well,
But I had to get rid of the lamp's awful smell,
And the muck all encrusted the length of its spout,
Yet as soon as I rubbed it I let out a shout,

For a loud bang erupted, and (was this a joke?)
My abode was engulfed in a thick cloud of smoke,
Which had cleared in a flash, leaving nothing behind
But a strange little man, clad in clothes of a kind

That they wore in the Orient during the time
Of Aladdin, in days of the old pantomime.....
"Who are you?" was my query, when speech had returned;
"I'm a genie," he answered, "and what you have earned

"Upon rubbing the lantern and summoning me
"Is a grant of three wishes – so what'll they be?"
"I could hardly believe it! My dreams had come true!
"How I wish I'd some *Tizer* to offer to you!"

(While pretending to act the congenial host
I was choosing which goodies I wanted the most.....)
"Hurry up!" he said grumpily, "Why the delay?
"Kindly spit out your wishes! I've not got all day!"

"Well, I wish you'd stop rushing me, please," I replied,
Trying hard to think quickly, to keep him onside;
"Listen up, crabby Genie, my wish number one
"Is for West Bromwich Albion to score goals for fun,

"And to win all their matches, and not lose a game,
"Retromingent on Arsenal, and Man U the same!
"Now my wish number two, if it falls within bounds,
"Is for millions, and billions, and trillions of pounds,

"All in bundles of fivers, though tens will be fine –
"I will even take twenties as my bottom line.
"For my third wish," I simpered, as confidence grew,
"I want that Clémence Posy and Léa Seydoux

"To come round in their undies, for *Tizer*, and stuff….."
"Hang about!" said the genie, "I've heard quite enough,
"For if what you have told me is really your dream
"I'll make West Bromwich Albion champions supreme,

"But I've told you before it's **THREE** wishes you've got,
"And you've had two already – so that one's your lot!"
"Why, you devious chiseller!" I bellowed, "What gall!
"I was promised three wishes but had none at all!"

"Yes you *have*," he exploded. "Remember the first?
"You wished for some *Tizer* to slake off my thirst!
"And then when, politely, I chivvied for haste,
"You wished I'd stop rushing you! (Bit of a waste

"Of a wish, if you ask me, but that's up to you!)
"So there's only one left – you've already had two….."
Well, to argue was pointless – he wasn't the type
To have listened to reason or hear out my gripe,

And besides, I had thought up the *cunningest* plan
To completely bamboozle this odious man,
And to get all I wanted, with wishes galore –
All the three I was promised, then hundreds, and more…..

"Very well," I said slyly, "this one wish will do:
"Just forget all the others – **I WISH I WERE YOU**!"
Now the genie looked puzzled by what I had said,
And I knew that my ruse had gone over his head.

But then, shrugging his shoulders, he simply said: "Done!
"Now you've had all your wishes and so I must run!"
And he vanished from view leaving nothing behind
But an odour of sulphur and cordite combined…..

You may feel I was crazy to want to be him
But my thinking was artful, and not just a whim,
For although it was clammy, and murky and damp,
You could do a lot worse than reside in the lamp,

Out of range of the nagging, and hidden from view,
Either drunk or asleep, in serene p & q,
With free access to magic whenever you choose
To accumulate moolah, or floozies, or booze…..

But although I outwitted the genie that day
I have lots of *musguvungs* that cause me *dusmay*,
'Cos the dream's gone to *ratshut* – my football team too –
And *U* still haven't had any *wushes* come true…..

*U* would love to say more, for *U*'ve much more to tell,
But my *typewruter*'s *startung* to play up as well…..

*December 2016*

# PALAVER[5]

A Happy Christmas and New Year,
And all that old palaver;
I shall not cease to wish you well
Till I am a cadaver.

*December, 1990*

---

[5] Written for my daughter, when she was a first-year medical student.

# MISSING YOU, AT CHRISTMAS

A long and painful Christmas Eve has ended,
Another lonely year has hirpled by,
And, though they say least said is soonest mended,
I can't believe you never said goodbye.

But when you left me not a word was spoken,
You slipped away as if our ties were sheared;
And though you must have known my heart was broken,
Without a backward glance, you disappeared.

But I could see you'd soon regret your leaving,
And that for me your heart would surely yearn;
You couldn't live without me without grieving,
And so you'd seek a pretext to return.

I must confess I'd not anticipated
That you would be so slow to find a way,
So every Christmas Eve since then I've waited,
Convinced that you'd be back by Christmas Day.

For it was Christmas Eve when I first met you,
Aboard the six-four-nine at Ponder's End;
I knew at once that I could not forget you,
That you would soon be more than just a friend.

We met the year the Spurs had won the double,
Bill Nicholson in charge of their campaign –
The year West Brom went on to prick their bubble
By beating them 2-1 at White Hart Lane.

How did a lad of fourteen football seasons
Win *you* – a wench of twenty-six or -eight?
But love is blind, and never offers reasons:
Our trolleybus adventure sealed your fate.

That night the bus was packed with party-poppers,
Whose noisy wives wore irritating smiles;
And all the rest were tired Christmas shoppers,
Whose parcels crammed the seats and blocked the aisles.

The trolleybus had room for standing only,
Though I'd got on ahead and found a seat,
But I was feeling miserable and lonely
Till you contrived a way for us to meet:

The sudden squeal of brakes at which you stumbled,
That pitched you – legs akimbo – in my lap,
And brought the brief apology you mumbled;
You fell – but I had fallen in your trap.

You knew that when our eyes met I was smitten,
Foreseeing I was yours and you were mine,
And (though you tried to hide it) we'd been bitten
By that old love bug on the six-four-nine.

No Tristan loved Isolde in this fashion;
No greater love did Romeo discharge;
No Pyramus craved Thisbe with such passion;
No Homer's heart beat louder for his Marje.

My fevered brain was suddenly a-flurry;
I groped for words to get my message right;
But when the bus stopped, you, in all your hurry,
Just scampered off, and vanished in the night.

That was – *alas!* – our one and only meeting,
And in a twinkling you had cut and run,
But, though for us the joys of love were fleeting,
For fifty years you've been the only one.

Affairs of heart are tortuous and weighty,
While broken dreams are difficult to mend,
But, though by now you must be pushing eighty,
It's time to bring your torment to an end.

I've tried to make it easier to find me,
As up to now your searching's been in vain,
So, leaving all my worldly goods behind me,
I've moved my dwelling close to your domain.

My home's a cardboard box on Tramway Avenue,
Pitched near the bus-stop where you done me wrong;
So come on, love, *for Chrissake*, let's be 'aving you!
Come back to me at once where you belong!

*December 2014*

# A FUSSY EATER? ME?

I am partial to a pheasant, and consider partridge pleasant,
Tasting not unlike the widgeon, or the Andalusian pigeon –
Please don't think me queer…….
I am willing to try eagle (at a pinch I'd eat a beagle),
So although this topic's tricky, and you're bound to call me picky,
Will you think it rather quirky if I ask you to leave turkey
Off my plate this year?
I am fond of fennec fox, and just a whiff of prairie oxen
Sees me dream of sprouts and gravy, while the Patagonian cavy
Makes a meal a feast;
I am not averse to otter, and I must confess I've got a
Subtle weakness for baked emu, curried coypu, peppered zebu,
Not forgetting hare, or horse, or porpoise, tortoise, bear
        (of course) or
Yummy wildebeest.
Pygmy hippo is my buddy! I don't mind if he leaves muddy
Footprints all across the lino, and the same goes for the rhino,
And the marabou;
Every mongoose, moose and sable's very welcome at my table,
As is wallaby and panda, even cow knob salamander,
Yet there's none whose flesh is sweeter than the spiny-backed
        anteater,
Or the caribou.
I am conscious that the llama (like the conch) is quite a charmer,
When he's stuffed with sage and lizard, till it's spilling out his
        gizzard,
And I just adore
The aroma of roast camel….! Every reptile, mollusc, mammal….!
Such as bradypus, or platypus, or octopus, or moggy puss, or
Stegosaurus, barosaurus, pterosaur or brontosaurus…..
But I like skunk more.

I'm a lover of grilled plover, and I really love to cover
Griffon vulture chicks with dripping from a chimp whose heart's
    still skipping,
And then wolf them whole!
Nothing beats okapi, bar an oven-ready capybara,
'Nless you find me a dead dodo, or a dragon from Komodo,
Or a fossa, or chinchilla, or a silverback gorilla,
Or a halal mole.
Serve me bucketloads of wombat! fruit bat! bobcat! polecat! tomcat!
Gosh! I don't know if I'm fonder of the quail or anaconda,
Or the kangaroo;
Never fob me off with duck, for I don't give a flying fox for
Any chicken-fowl or paltry lesser form of galline poultry,
But I betcha I could scoff a lot of porcupine and oce-
Lot, and certainly I'd eat a bally jungleful of cheetah,
Leopards, lemurs, lions, lynxes, monkeys, marmosets and minks (es-
Pecially!) parrots, pumas, puppies, gophers, goats, giraffes and
    guppies,
Donkey, dolphin, indri, dingo, dromedary and (by jingo!)
Kiwi, kakapo and cattle, hake, and caracal, and rattle-
Snake, koala bear, and (maybe) armadillo, or bush-baby,
Hoopoe, Whooper swan, or husky, hedgehog, ptarmigan, or tusky
Tiger, Tom's gazelle, or fawn – I will eat **ANY** sodding fauna!
I love dugong, bongo, beaver, aye aye, cuscus, dik dik, drever,
So I've no idea why it must be your turkey every Christmas,
When you know I'm simply clemming for a bellyful of lemming,
Or of gerbil, or of mandrill – feed me road kill!! – even pigswill!!! –
And I positively slaver for the doggy Shih Tzu flavour
That identifies each sliver of his offal, lights and liver,
And the thought of Congo River's scrummy crocs just makes me
    shiver.....!
Now, my taste buds are a-quiver – so if Waitrose won't deliver
Just try Whipsnade Zoo.

*December 2013*

# GHOST STORY

I went to bed one Christmas Eve, and fell asleep, and dreamed
That it was time for cocoa, prayers, and bed, or so it seemed,
And, puzzled, put my jimmies on again, and went to bed
A second time that Christmas night; but barely had my head
Compressed the pillow when the room was bathed in eerie light,
And I could sense a spooky presence cowering out of sight.
"Has Santa come?" I asked myself. "I hope he finds my
       stocking!"
But I was whistling in the dark; the truth was far more shocking.....

A wintry draught caressed my cheek before my eyes were op'ed;
Then, turmoil spinning in my head, I felt my withers groped
By icy fingers creeping upward through my inner thigh,
Till, at the point of no return, I could not stay a cry
Of anguish: "Santa! Whoa! Enough! I beg of you, refrain!
"I'm but a poor boy, timid, weak and blessed with little brain."
But Father Christmas wasn't there – my guesswork was in error;
A ghostly maid stood by my bed, whose gaze filled me with terror.....

Her eye was wild, her face was fierce, but her attire was scanty:
No coat, no frock, no vest, no sock, no brassiere, no panty;
But any hope she might be up for playing trains and tunnels
Was scuppered when she opened up both barrels from the
       gunwales.
"**BE MUCH AFRAID!**" the spectre cried, "for I am sent from
       hell,
"To punish reprobates like thee, wherever they may dwell!
"So spare me thy pretend remorse of guilty deed compunctive,
"For I'm the Ghost of Christmas Past Anterior Subjunctive!

"I come to castigate the bad and maximise their fears;
"My mission usually lasts all night – with thee it may take years!
"For, since thou art the very worst, behold Apocalypse,
"Bespoke with red hot pincers, screws, the rack, and flails and
        whips!"
When I awoke my throat was dry, my jimmies soaked in sweat;
The nightmare seemed so very real the memory lingers yet.
Though still not certain what the Dickens this was all about,
I screamed in horror, knowing I was truly up the spout.

So I decided then and there to take no further chances,
And rid my life of vice and crime and all extravagances,
In case the phantom spoke the truth and sin comes back to hurt you;
That's why I stand before you now, a paragon of virtue.
Yet still I'm troubled..... Was I mad to quit when I was winning?
Was she for real? Had I been duped? Could I have gone on sinning?
I can't explain these nagging doubts – don't ask me to attempt it –
But, did I dream I was asleep? Or had I dreamed I'd dreamt it?

*December 2012*

3 2

# A CHILD'S CHRISTMAS WISH.....

Dear Santa, Please bring lots of toys,
The kind of things that little boys
Can play with all the long day through –
I'll leave the detail up to you.

But Santa, while I have your ear,
Why do you come just once a year?
I think it would be rather swell
If you came Guy Fawkes Day, as well!

And New Year's Day, and Hallowe'en,
And all the Wednesdays in between,
And Whitsun, Easter, April, May.....
Dear Santa, please come every day!

*December, 2011*

# BIRTHDAY WORMS

# THE FIBBER

The passing years have always been
A mystery to me;
When I was born, for instance, you
Were very nearly three.

When I was ten, you were sixteen –
A little girl no more!
But now I'm forty-six, while you
Are only thirty-four.

*circa 1991*

# SIXTY YEARS YOUNG[6]

Oh, how I wish I was sixty!
If I were everything would be fine!
Oh, what I'd give to be sixty, but
I'm still only fifty-nine…..

*February 2007*

---

[6] Written on the occasion of an elderly friend's sixtieth birthday.

# EIGHTY YEARS YOUNG[7]

It is ever so nice to be eighty!
Why does everyone make such a fuss?
People think what you say is so weighty,
And they give you their seat on the bus!

When you're sixty life's full of frivolity,
And your body may feel free of pain,
But at eighty life's so full of jollity,
And you don't have to stand on the train!

Though your blood pressure's constantly racing,
And you're turning to mutton from lamb,
And your knees and your hips need replacing,
People give up their seat on the tram!

Well, OK – you may not be mobile,
And you'll spend much more time in your bed,
And you've no chance with anything nubile,
So you make do with cocoa instead.

But the downs are outweighed by the pluses,
And your neighbours all treat you so nice,
And they give you their seats on the buses,
And they let you say everything twice.

So, a Happy Big Birthday to Brenda,
Who will no longer live like a monk…
(I just heard her tell the bartender,
From today she'll be permanently drunk…)

---

[7] Written on the occasion of a youthful friend's eightieth birthday.

For, apart from the boils and the flatulence,
And the scabies, the itch and the runs,
And the cataracts, piles and incontinence,
Being eighty's just oodles of fun! (ZZzzzzzz…..)

*February 2021*

# JAILHOUSE ROCK

Oh crumbs! Oh Crikey! Mama mia!
I fear it is that time of year,
When I consult the Muse immortal
In search of bumf to make you chortle.

I'd meant to pen a birthday rhyme
But now I haven't got the time;
I've left it far too late, you see,
What with the housework, down to me:
The cooking, cleaning of the loo,
And gardening – I do that too –
And making beds, and scrubbing floors,
And all the other household chores,
And making cakes, and darning socks,
And serving whisky on the rocks
To 'er indoors, who stays in bed
Till work is over – 'nough said.

I haven't bought you any present,
Or anything that's half as pleasant,
But I believe, though could be wrong,
The greatest gift's the gift of song,
So no big prezzie, as I've said,
But what I'm going to do instead
Is sink a bottle or two of Hock,
Then sing a verse of *Jailhouse Rock*,
And though you'll be denied the pleasure
Of hearing it in fullest measure,
For you'll be *there*, and I'll be *here*,
There is no need to shed a tear –
You'll *know*, round about half-past two,
That I'll be singing it for you!

*circa 1988*

40

# SOUND ADVICE

*Psst!!!* Mr Doddles!!! I hear it's her birthday, but
Money is short and your back's to the wall.
Want my advice on the way to get over it?
Sort out the housekeeping once and for all?
**DON'T BREATHE A WORD,** not to Ann or the progeny,
Or to the Jockey Club down at the course.
Somebody told me you're fond of a flutter, so
Let's get a paper and pick us a horse!

Don't take no notice of tipsters or oracles;
Winks from a trainer are just for the mug;
Betting on favourites will not make you rich enough…
(Hush! Not a word to the lads in the snug!)
**THOUSAND TO ONE SHOT** is what you are looking for –
Form that's appalling, and eyesight the same!
Broken, and winded, and fat as an elephant,
Coughing, and sweating, and (preferably) lame!

Mortgage your house, and your family's inheritance –
Don't tell your bankers in case they foreclose –
Sell all your valuables, pensions and policies;
Two or three million must go on the nose!!!!!
Once the bet's on you will feel a lot chirpier –
Large gin and tonics till racing begins!
Yes, if it loses will take some explaining, but
Lord God Almighty, John – **WHAT IF IT WINS**!!!!!!!!!!!!!!!

*1995*

# AIDE-MÉMOIRE

My memory is very bad;
I can't remember what I had
For breakfast; nor can I recall
My lunch, or if I ate at all,
And, when the Albion lose, I swear
I can't remember why I care.
I also keep forgetting dates,
Like all the birthdays of my mates,
And though I try so very hard
I never think to send a card.

My tattooist knew what to do:
He said the answer was tattoo,
And said I would avoid disgrace
If all the dates were on my face,
Then took a needle to my skin,
And quickly inked the key dates in,
But *backwards* did the words engrave
So I'm reminded when I shave!

Now birthdays are no longer missed,
For, even when I'm *Brahms and Liszt*,
I always will remember yours,
And all my kids', and 'ers indoors,
And, though I may look quite a sight,
I never miss a Bonfire Night,
Or New Year's Day, or Hallowe'en,
Or any knees-up in between,
So all my woes are in the past,
And I have found true peace at last.

*circa 1990*

42

# GBH

Your birthday's here, and I just pray
That no one steals your cake away.
If someone causes such disgrace,
I hope you'll punch him in the face,
And bash his head against a tree,
And crush his privates with your knee,
And break his back, and crack his shin,
And gouge his eyes out with a pin,
And slit his nose with an electric saw,
And nail his todger to the floor;
Pour boiling treacle on his head,
And bayonet him until he's dead,
And finally burn him at the stake,
To teach him not to touch your cake,
And spoil your birthday's anniversary.
(I hope this violence won't be necessary.)

*2023*

# SORRY, BUT TODAY IS *MY* BIRTHDAY

I missed your call at seven,
But I'm having a lie in today;
I'm normally up by eleven,
But today I'm not moving till May.

*April, 2021*

# WORMS OF LOVE

# HAND GRENADE

My love is like a hand grenade
With loosely fitting pin;
Sometimes I find it's fallen out
When I thought it was in.

I live with danger every day,
But never get the hang
Of living with a hand grenade.
All's tickety-boo, then… Bang!!!!!!!!!!!!!!!

*December, 1981*

# BLOOD THINNERS

I feed my cat on *Warfarin*,
Which he thinks is a joke;
I'm trying to protect his health,
But he would like a stroke.

My moggy means a lot to me;
I hope he leaves me never;
I'll love him till the cows come home,
But I'll love you for ever.

*December 2022*

# GOLF CLUB

In the diner at the golf club, far away from all the hubbub
That disturbs the peace on every Christmas Eve,
At a quiet, secluded table, sat a slightly sozzled Mabel,
Munching luncheon with her husband, heart on sleeve.

But their festive manducation was no routine celebration
Just of Christmas, for December twenty-four
Was their wedding anniversary, and no evil vibe precursory
Could destroy the perfect joy of one year more.

Everyone who knew them noted they were very much devoted
To each other, though the years had simply flown;
They shared all the household jobbies, even tried each other's
        hobbies,
And were happiest when together, left alone.

There was never any stressing – she could simply count her
        blessings,
And rejoice that he and she were kindred souls;
They did everything together, and, in any kind of weather,
Every week they'd play a round of eighteen holes.

Thirty years they had been wedded, and she knew this
        level-headed
Guy was all she could have wished for through the years;
Merest hint of his devotion triggered welling of emotion
That was quite enough to move the lass to tears.

And she'd sunk a lot of bubbly, the effect of which had doubly
Piqued the maudlin muse, and made her catch her breath;
Boughs of mistletoe and holly couldn't shift the melancholy
Rumination, which had turned her thoughts… to death.

"Though I know how much I'm cherished, dearest darling, if
        I perished,
"And without me you were forced to spend your life…
"Though I know you'd be heartbroken, and she'd only be a token,
"Could you bring yourself to take another wife?"

Well, that called for some reflection, and it put a new complexion
On proceedings that till now had seen her purr;
If he said: "No, don't be soppy!" would that simply make her
        stroppy?
Might she see it as a judgement call on *her*?

Well aware that careless talk would have a way of turning awkward,
He was thinking fast but feigning nonchalance;
Yet while paying full attention he could feel a note of tension
Creeping in as she awaited his response.

So, some fleeting hesitation, then the self-congratulation
Due an answer that had not been born of haste:
"Yes, I might, *Blancmange!* – but only to prevent me feeling lonely,
"For you know, *My Sausage! – you* can't be replaced!"

If she'd parked it there, and waited till her skittishness abated,
P'raps the magic of before could be restored,
But the fact that she was squiffy made her judgement somewhat iffy,
So she pressed the point that she had just explored.

"Would you give her my new sable?" wondered hyper-focused
        Mabel,
"My designer frocks, and all my other clothes?"
Feeling very much afraid he might offload on a new lady,
She protested: "You just *couldn't* give her those!"

"Well, I *might*," he now conceded, "if a use for them were needed,
"Otherwise the moths would only chew 'em through;
"But this new imagin-*ary* woman I'm supposed to marry
"Wouldn't ever look as good in them as you!

"But you mustn't get hysterical over something hypothetical,"
He continued, eager now to stem her flow;
"Your surreal imagination is just causing aggravation –
"You should leave it out..." But would she listen? *No!*

"What about my rocks and jewels, and the rest of life's accruals,
"Like my necklaces and bracelets – *ruddy hell!* –
"Surely you'd not make arrangement for my ring from our
        engagement...?
"*Lawks-a-mercy!* You'd not give her that as well?"

But by now he'd found a rhythm: "Well, what *else* would I do
        with 'em?
"Couldn't leave 'em lying idle in a drawer...!
"So, I guess, maybe I'd share 'em, and if she should ever
        wear 'em,
"I would miss you, *Pumpkin Pie*, a whole lot more!"

"But, when out to woo and win her, you would not come *here* to
        dinner,
"To our favourite eating house in all the land?
"To this place we've venerated, which to us is almost sacred...
"You *can't* bring her here – what don't you understand?"

"Well, I wouldn't do it lightly," he extemporised politely,
"But my friends are here, and this is where we meet,
"So if *they* made reservations I'd accept their invitations –
"Though I'd only come because a man must eat!"

Still another whinge was dawning: "…And your gift to me this
    morning?
"If you gave her *that* you'd cut me with a knife!
"I would find it *most* unpleasant if my anniversary present
"Were to end up in the hands of your new wife!"

She found just the strength to splutter: "**<u>NOT</u>** my *Scotty Cameron*
    putter!
"Give her *that* and my remains would run amuck!!!!!"
"Not a chance!" he snorted, candid; "you're in luck there – *she's*
    *left-handed*…
"No, hang on a sec… I didn't mean… Oh *fiddlesticks*!"

*December 2020*

# YOU'RE WONDERFUL

You're wonderful, you're wondrous,
You're beautiful, you're marvellous,
You're my inspiration too;
You're gorgeous, and you're cuddly,
And you're stunning, and you're lovely,
And everything I do is for you.

You're Elgar, you're Mozart,
Le Musée des Beaux Arts,
You're the star at the top of the tree;
You're Oxford, you're Portsmouth,
You're Venus, you're Emsworth,
You're everything that's anything to me.

You are my cocaine, my heroin,
You're West Bromwich Albion,
You make me feel good when I feel bad;
You are my partner, my buddy,
My squaw and my caddie,
And you're the best friend that I ever had.

You're Beaujolais, you're camembert,
You're Bouchard – le fils et le père –
You're Góngora, you're Calderón;
You're Vergil, you're Homer,
You're Browning, you're Zola,
You're everything that turns me on.

You are my partner, my soulmate,
My sweetheart, my bedmate,
My woman, my lover, my wife;
Please don't ever forget
That I love you, Colette,
And I shall love you for the rest of my life.

*circa 1966*

# ODE TO A LAMPPOST

I have fallen in love with a lamppost:
The one outside the pub, by the drains;
She stands proud and erect,
Winning instant respect,
Though she drips like a tap, when it rains.

2

I have asked Mistress Lamppost to marry me,
But she hasn't replied, so I guess
She's still thinking it over,
Yet I'll be in clover,
If she should decide to say yes.

3

I'm not sure why I fell for a lamppost,
But there must have been love in the air,
For as soon as I saw her
I dumped a chain saw… *Er…*
…With which I was having an affair…

4

…And this kind of thing runs in the family,
For my auntie's engaged to a tree,
While my wayward brother's
Significant other's
A traffic cone on the M3.

5

As my narcissist sister, Xenobia,
Was afraid she'd be left on the shelf,
When a dulcimer zither
Ignored her come-hither,
She elected to marry herself.

6

Then my cousin was summonsed for trigamy,
After plighting his troth to three pigs,
The same day as his daughter
Was spliced at the altar
To a bottle of syrup of figs.

7

But the light of *my* life is my lamppost!
She's so tall – at least eighteen foot three!
And she's frightfully bright
When she's turned on at night;
She's not dim as a dipstick, like me.

8

Yet my lamppost forgives my shortcomings,
Which are mega, immoral, and many;
So, it's difficult to see
What my lamp sees in me,
When in her I can find hardly any.

9

She is kind, she is gentle, she's loving,
While her character's upright and solid;
Though some joker maligned
Her stressed concrete behind,
And her perfume, which some might call 'olid'.

10[8]

The mephitic appeal of my sweetheart
Carries more than a *soupçon* of poo,
With a *frisson* of wee,
For, indecorously,
All the dogs use my love as a loo.

---

[8] Optional tenth stanza, perhaps best omitted when reciting at royal garden parties.

10/11

If her odour's not one to be sniffed at,
The extent of my ardour is cosmic;
So, it's right what they say,
At the end of the day,
That true love is both blind and anosmic.

11/12

I spend all day long hugging my lamppost,
And I've never yet found her unwilling,
Although some folks are shocked,
And one ding-a-ling mocked:
"You're eleven pence short of a shilling!"

12/13

But that doesn't mean that I'm barmy –
Saucy, *lamppostist* taunts are in vain;
I'm a postmodern convert,
Not a dirty old pervert,
So you'd better not call me insane,

13/14

Or I'll call out the local constabulary,
And I'll have *you* locked up, then you'll see
That, for all our reliance
On wisdom, and science,
The whole world's gone bananas – bar me!

*December 2023*

# PANTOMIME[9]

My girlfriend loves the pantomime – she drags me there each year;
She likes to climb up on her seat, and scream for all to hear,
And boo the villain, cheer the prince, and laugh, or shed a tear…
(I'd rather take her down the pub and fill her up with beer,
But if we miss the panto I just get it in the ear.)

Then this year lockdown intervened to scupper her demands:
"No pantomime for us!" I told her. "Number 10 commands
"Us all to keep our distance, or face fines and reprimands!
"We must protect the NHS – all England understands!
"I'll get a takeaway instead! Now go and wash your hands!"

She didn't take it lying down, but yelled till she was hoarse:
"That rotter Cummings did it just to spoil our intercourse!
"*I NEED MY PANTO FIX!!!*" she screamed, with
        monumental force,
"I want to see *Aladdin* – and it's on in Gerrards Cross!
"So, *book us tickets*! Otherwise – we're heading for divorce!"

Oh dear, my Christmas goose was cooked: the solids hit the fans…
I felt I'd fallen in the fire from out the frying pans…
My popularity with her was lower than Iran's
In Golder's Green. I needed strength to rival Superman's…
"OK," I sighed, "I'll do my best. Now go and wash your hands!"

If I'm to take her to that show, while social distancing,
I'll need the genie of the lamp to come and pull a string…
I've racked my brain for ages but come up with not a thing…
If we are seen together MI5 might mount a sting,
And she could be subjected to a frightful tasering…

---

[9] Written during Covid 19.

But then, while I was making light of countless lager cans,
The answer hoofed me up the kilt! I rang her with my plans:
"You head on up to Gerrards Cross with all *Aladdin* fans,
"While I am watching *Cinderella* down at Blackpool Sands –
"I've solved the problem at a stroke! Now go and wash your
        hands!"

While she's with Widow Twankey, I shall be down by the sea!
Two *different* shows in *different* towns on *different* nights!
        Whoopee!
That's distancing *par excellence*! Without hyperbole,
I thought she'd be ecstatic at my ingenuity…
But now she won't pick up the phone: she's washed her hands
        of me.

*December 2020*

# THANK GOODNESS

I can remember far off times
When life was filled with silly rhymes,
When aim was high, and care was small,
For I was young, and knew it all;
When life was run at hectic pace
And everything just fell in place,
And I could have whate'er I dreamed
Of, for the asking – so it seemed.

But suddenly a page has turned;
Now cash is spent before it's earned;
The questions linger as before,
But answers just won't come no more.
So many bridges still uncrossed,
And memory's not all I've lost:
Less eyesight, hearing, teeth and hair –
Thank goodness, love, that you're still there…

*December 1991*

# NUMBERS

One and one and one is three,
And one more one is four;
Another one, I think, is five –
My toes won't stretch to more.

Twenty-four is just one short,
But Christmas is a-coming;
Four by two's a bit of wood,
Twelve is drummers drumming.

Eighty-eight's two ladies, fat,
Two times four is eight;
205's for Hammond Street[10],
Half-past twelve is late.

Twelve less six is half a doz.,
A hundred is a ton;
Sixty-five's when Winston died,
Sixty-eight was fun[11].

Thirteen is a baker's doz.,
And Jaxon's birthday date;
Fifteen is the Ides of March,
Ten stone's welterweight.

---

[10] London Transport's route 205 used, I believe, to terminate at Hammond Street, in Cheshunt.

[11] West Bromwich Albion, I believe, won the FA Cup in 1968.

Sixty-six is clickety click,
Sixty-four's two fewer;
Eighty dead is boiling point,
*D'après* Réaumur.

Jimmy Greaves is number eight;
Forty-five's a gun;
Two and six is half a crown[12] –
But *you* are NUMBER ONE.

*circa 1967*

---

[12] Twelve and a half pence, for those too young to remember.

# PRUDENCE

Bonjour, Prudence; reste avec moi;
J'aurai toujours besoin de toi.
Sois toujours ma meilleure amie :
N' m' laiss' pas faire de conneries.

Je t'aime, Prudence; reste à côté,
Et ne me quitte plus jamais ;
Ne me fais jamais de soucis ;
Reste avec moi, je t'en supplie.

Comment, Prudence ? Dis donc ! Arrête !
Ça fait longtemps que tu m'embêtes !
La garce ! Putain ! Vieil elephant !
Fiche-moi la paix ! Va ! Fous le camp !

*1989*

# WORMS FOR THE KIDS

# THE GOLDFISH

Of all the birds that God has wrought
The goldfish is the oddest.
His beak is soft, his wings are short,
His plumage earns a score of nought,
And, unlike what you may have thought,
His singing voice is modest.

He's not a turkey, or a rook –
His bill resembles neither.
I've had a very careful look
In every library reference book
And found, unless I'm much mistook,
He's not an either eider.
(*Er..... sorry.* He's not an eider either.)

I've hardly ever seen him fly -
The effort gets him flustered.
His take-off stride is all awry,
He seldom gets above knee-high,
In fact, he doesn't even try -
The lazy little bustard[13]!

Oh God! What hast Thou got to say?
He's no idea of nesting!
Didst Thou throw Genesis away
And, all shagged out, when tempers fray,
Create him on the seventh day,
When Thou shouldst have been resting?

---

[13] For the avoidance of doubt, it should perhaps be pointed out that the little bustard (*tetrax tetrax*) is a bird in the bustard family.

My goldfish drives me in a rage!!!!!!!!!
From morn to afternoon, he
Won't eat his millet, or engage
His little swing. At every stage
He flops about the floor of his cage,
And treats **me** like a loony!!!!!!!!!

*circa 1985*

# CATFOOD

I have a brand new kitten;
I think he's rather nice,
But don't know what to feed him on:
Can you give me advice?

        I feed *my* cat on dustbin scraps
        And mouldy bread untasted.
        He doesn't like the flavour, but
        It stops it being wasted.

        I feed *my* cat on *Ajax*,
        Which I keep on his shelf;
        He doesn't like the flavour, but
        He cleans his tray himself.

        I feed *my* cat on shower-gel,
        Which ends up in his belly.
        He doesn't like the flavour, but
        *His* litter-tray's not smelly!

        I feed *my* cat on scraps of wool,
        Because he knows no better;
        I empty out his tray with care
        In case he s… knits a sweater.

        I feed *my* cat on cannabis,
        And hash, and LSD.
        He doesn't like the flavour, yet
        He flies home for his tea.

        I feed *my* cat testosterone –
        The ideal food for cheaters!
        He doesn't like the flavour, but
        He won the hundred metres.

I feed *my* cat on caviar
As if he were a nob;
He doesn't like the flavour,
But then, I'm a frightful snob.

I feed *my* cat on cigarettes
And dust from baccy pouches.
He doesn't like the flavour, but
My wife collects the vouchers.

I feed *my* cat on dog poo
And fetid matters *putral*;
He doesn't like the flavour, but
I think it's carbon neutral.

I feed *my* cat on *Paxo* –
He isn't very chuffed;
He clearly doesn't like it, but
I've told him to get stuffed.

I feed *my* cat on…

I'm really grateful to you all
For what you've had to say;
I'll think on it, and let you know,
Perhaps, another day…..

*circa 1975*

# MAX'S CHRISTMAS

On Christmas Day young Max awoke
To hear the sound of bells;
Then suddenly he heard a thud
Followed by anguished yells.
It seemed to come from up on high
And when he peeked outside,
Old Santa Claus was on the roof
With reindeer on the slide!

"Oh, Max!" cried Santa, "I'm so pleased
"To see you at this juncture,
"For as my sleigh came down to land,
"Old Rudolph sprung a puncture!
"I must deliver all these gifts
"By early Christmas Morn,
"But I can't get a vet in time
"To finish before dawn!

"The good news is I'm nearly done –
"But *nearly* is not quite!
"The bad news is I've two more towns
"To do before it's light!"
"Don't worry, Santa," shouted Max,
"I'll help you if I can!"
"Hush up!" said Santa, "Not so loud!
"Try not to wake up Dan!

4

"But if you're quiet you can help me

"If you're feeling kind."

"Sorry," Max whispered, very soft,

"What did you have in mind?"

"Take half these toys," Santa explained,

"And then, my little friend,

"I'll finish off in Highgate here

"If you could do Crouch End."

5

"How will I get there?" Max enquired,

"It's rather far to go."

"Don't worry, I've a bike for you

"To ride there through the snow!"

So Max took half the toys with him

And rode down Hornsey Lane,

Up past his school, and through the town,

As fast as any train!

6

Delivering toys to every house

Wherein a child resides –

A game for him, a doll for her,

And plenty more besides,

Until at last his work was done,

And then he homeward sped,

And waved goodbye to Santa

Before toddling back to bed.

7

Then back at school in January,
In class, in 'Show and tell',
A little girl with toys to show,
Had quite a tale as well:
"I caught a glimpse, on Christmas Night,
"Of Santa, with his sacks,
"And, you will not believe this, but –
"Santa looks just like Max!"

*December, 2011*

# AMY'S SIXTH BIRTHDAY

Why have I put a cross inside
My diary for today?
Is it because it's Christmas, or
The Easter holiday?
Must we take Bella to the vet?
Is something on TV?
Am I to have special treat,
Like *All Bran* for my tea?
Can there be something I must do,
Or someone I must meet?
Can it be time to cut my hair,
Or time to wash my feet?
I can't remember what it is.
Oh dear! I'm in a fix.
But… Wait a minute!! I remember!!
Amy Helen's SIX!!!!!

*May, 1983*

# THE FAT CAT

My moggy shares my every meal –
He always eats with me;
At breakfast-time he tastes my toast
And then he drinks my tea.

He thinks my lunch is just for him,
And gobbles up my ham;
And tea-time finds him on my lap –
He loves my bread and jam.

My dinner is just ecstasy,
(For him, I mean, not me).
He hoovers up my meat and greens,
And then waits patiently

Till half-past ten, and supper-time,
He's back for cheese on toast,
Washed down with Beaujolais, or Hock
(He likes this meal the most!)

I'm growing thinner day by day,
While he's just growing fat.
Thank God he's off his *Whiskas* though –
At least he leaves me that…..

*circa 1985*

# CHRISTMAS PUD

I baked myself a Christmas pud,
With twenty pound coins in it,
My dog came in and wolfed the lot
In under half a minute;
To find the coins I pumped his tum,
But can't deny the rumours
That all I got was thirty p,
And a pair of ladies' bloomers.

*December 2023*

# DAN'S CHRISTMAS

Father Christmas said to Dan:
"Let it be understood,
"I've *lots* of lovely toys for you –
"But *only* if you're good!"

"I <u>*have*</u> been good!" young Dan replied.
Said Father Christmas: "Blimey!
"In that case you can have the toys –
"But first you must untie me!"

*December, 2010*

# DODDLES[14]

I don't ask very much from life,
I am a simply bloke;
I'd rather have a little puss
Whose fleece was grey as smoke
Than any *MR2 Mark I*
Or any later models…
And you can call him what you like
But I will call him 'Doddles'.

*1993*

---

[14] Written when my children wanted me to rechristen our new little grey kitten, which I had named after a friend.

# TABLE MANNERS

My grandson, who is nearly two
Has caused a dreadful how d'ye-do
Because I told him to his face-full
His table manners were disgraceful.

He'd filled his face with ham and chips,
Then squeezed some grapes between his lips,
Then crammed some chocolate past his chin,
Then tried to force a sausage in!

Then, like a minor concrete mixer,
His jaws compacted this elixir,
To which he'd added a fruit bun;
But, as of yet, he'd swallowed none.

And then he spoke! Through jowls juiceful,
He begged me to do something useful.
With cheeks so bulging they must ache,
Spit-speckled, splashed, he spluttered: "Cake?"

I pointed sternly to the mess,
And asked him why he'd no finesse.
Wide-eyed, he pointed out with glee:
'Twas all inherited from me!

*circa January, 2006*

# AN ECOLOGICAL NIGHTMARE[15]

There's a little town in Sweden
Where there dwells a man called Lars,
Whose hobbies include pickling fruit,
And bottling it in jars,
But who by trade's a lumberjack;
He keeps his axe well honed;
He chopped a tree down Wednesday night,
And then went and got stoned.

At the bottom of the ocean
Dwelt a colony of squids;
There was Roger, the big daddy one,
Then Martha, and the kids.
Last Wednesday night some fisher folk
Had Martha for their suppers,
But they brought Roger back to land
And stored him near the scuppers.

Young Simon is a clever lad,
The pride of Mrs Connors:
She sent him up to Oxford, where
He got a fourth (with honours).
And now he runs his father's firm:
He heats small plastic cubes;
He drills them, rolls and stretches them,
To make small plastic tubes.

---

[15] Written on the occasion of a family wedding.

Remember Lars? On Thursday morn
A shocking head he had,
But he was up at crack of noon,
And, aided by his dad,
He cut his tree up into logs,
And sent them off to Wien,
Where Eberhard von Schnittenwurst
Possessed a big machine.

Ex-convict though he may have been,
Old Eberhard is now
A well respected businessman
With fat and homely Frau.
(She gives him lots of Wurst to eat:
He downs it at one gulp.)
He threw Lars' logs in his machine
And ground them into pulp.

Meanwhile, those fisher folk had grabbed
Old Roger – legs a-dangle –
And shoved and strained till they had forced
Poor Roger through a mangle!
They strained his innards, and the juice
Was carefully stored in jars,
Which, by irrelevant perchance
Had once belonged to Lars!

Man cannot live by bread alone:
Export's a better way.
So thought von Schnittenwurst, at least,
And so, without delay,
His quick-dried pulp, now smooth and flat,
He sent to Angleterre.
And Roger's bottled essence, too,
By chance, was posted there.

Syd Clodgett made great piles of cash,
To his eternal glory.
(The painful piles he suffered from
Were quite another story.)
'Twas at his firm, where pens are made,
From lengthened plastic cubes,
That Roger's last remains were squeezed
In one of Simon's tubes.

And so reflect. You are to blame!
Ecologists agree!
Did Roger have to die that way?
And what of Lars's tree?
Was all that really justified?
I'm simply asking whether
Environments should be destroyed
Just so that I can sit down and use pen, paper and ink to express
        our sincere hope that you will enjoy the best of health and
        happiness for ever and ever together?

*April, 1979*

# SPEECH TRAINING[16]

Of all the things I like the best
My kitten is the faithfullest;
There's such a lot that you can do
Together, just your puss and you.
For instance, you can play at chase,
Or hide and seek, or have a race,
Or you can take him for a walk,
Or you can teach him how to talk.
(How dare you scoff! Just mark my words -
It's easier than catching birds!)
Or he will help you catch a mouse,
Or he will help you paint the house -
Just dip his withers in the pot -
A splendid paintbrush you have got!
Yes, there's no end to what he'll do
Simply to prove his love for you.
He'll help you clean the sink and bath,
Or build a crazy paving path,
Or wash the car, or drain the lake,
Or help you bake a birthday cake
(So you can have a birthday treat)
And hold the candles in his feet.
Just poke them in between his toes
Or in his ears, or up his nose,
Or any orifice. You'll find
The faithful kitten will not mind,
And if he does, who cares? Recall:
He's just a kitten, after all,

---

[16] No children or animals were discommoded during the excretion of this piece of doggerel (please see page 11), but on no account should any of the advice offered here be followed when attempting to teach animals to talk.

So if he wants to make a fuss
Who gives a monkey's? Bah! Not us!
So shove those candles where you will!
Bore holes with your electric drill,
And drive them in! And if that fails
Just wedge them up his fingernails!
And LIGHT THE WICKS! Tee hee, don't balk!
We'll make the little bustard[17] talk!

*circa 1985*

_____

[17] A little bustard is a bird. Remember? See page 64.

# PUT YOUR TEETH IN, MAX[18]!

*Teeth in Max, teeth in Max,*
*Put your teeth in, Max.*
*Teeth in Max, teeth in Max,*
*Put your teeth in Max.*

Put your teeth in, Max,
Or you'll find your favourite snacks
Will just ooze between the cracks
Of your gums, and slither back.
Put your teeth in, Max,
'Cos we want you to relax,
But we don't want people thinking you're a slob.

Chorus
*Teeth in Max, teeth in Max,*
*Put your teeth in, Max.*
*Teeth in Max, teeth in Max,*
*Put your teeth in Max.*

Put your teeth in, Max,
When you blow your tenor-sax
Or the people at the back
Will all have to wear their macs.
Put your teeth in, Max,
And forget your paddywhacks,
'Cos we don't you behaving like a yob.

---

[18] Written at a time before young Max was old enough to have grown any teeth.

<u>Chorus</u>
*Teeth in Max, teeth in Max,*
*Put your teeth in, Max.*
*Teeth in Max, teeth in Max,*
*Put your teeth in Max.*

Put your teeth in, Max
Or I'll send your mum a fax
And suggest she gives you smacks
On the bottom of your slacks
To remind you of the facts
That your manners are too lax
And you haven't put your choppers in your gob.

<u>Final Chorus</u>
*Teeth in Max, teeth in Max,*
*Put your teeth in, Max!*
*Teeth in Max, teeth in Max,*
*Put your teeth in Max!*

*circa 2005*

# AMY HELEN, AMY HELEN

*Refrain*
*Amy Helen, Amy Helen,*
*You're a lovely little girl,*
*Amy Helen, Amy Helen,*
*And you've got me in a whirl;*
*From the botton[19] of your botton*
*To your eyes of shiny blue,*
*Amy Helen, Amy Helen,*
*I love every inch of you.*

You were born in Solihull General
On a dull and cloudy day,
But as soon as you were born, love,
All the black clouds blew away.
Though the thunder often thunders,
And there's often lightning too,
Amy Helen, Amy Helen,
It will never rain on you.

*Refrain*

---

[19] Translator's note. A polite word for "bottom", invented by daughter number one after the birth of daughter number two.

Though you're sometimes very naughty
I will let you off for years,
'Cos there's sunshine in your laughter
But there's heartbreak in your tears.
You're the baddest little baby
That God ever sent to Earth,
But I love you ever so, Amy,
I cannot estimate your worth.

*Refrain*

*circa June, 1977*

# DR CHEESECAKE[20] JOBSHARES

Christmas morn found Father Christmas,
Busily delivering toys,
Carefully filling every stocking,
For those sleeping girls and boys.
With his helper and his reindeer,
He'd been up throughout the night,
Tired, but feeling very happy,
For the end was now in sight.
"Phew!" gasped Santa, puff and blowing,
"This gets harder every year!"
Flopping down upon a rooftop,
Wiping soot out of his ear,
"Are we nearly finished, Cheesey?
"Are there many more to go?
"That last chimney nearly killed me –
"I'm too old for his, you know!"
Dr Cheesecake pricked his ears up,
Holding on to Rudolph's head,
Just to stop himself from sliding,
"I'm as whacked as you!" he said.
"Toys get heavier every Christmas!"
Then he ticked off Santa's list,
"I think we are nearly finished –
"Let's just see who we have missed.
"Vera's had her new leg-warmers…"

---

[20] For many years my daughters believed that Santa's principal helper was Dr Cheesecake, a medically qualified elf who specialised in the treatment of chilblains, frostbite, hypothermia, trench foot, chapped lips and other arctic ailments. They were in their thirties before they discovered that, although Santa was very real, Dr Cheesecake was but a figment of my imagination.

Santa broke in, with a grin:
"I have filled them up with apples –
"How will she get her legs in?"
"Lucy's had a new recorder,
"Amy's got a rubber duck;
"Jane got *Cluedo*, Bobby *Ludo*,
"Billy got some sweets to suck."
"That's the lot, then," said old Santa,
"There's just that house on the hill;
"Let me see now, Susie's tights and
"Percy's smelly socks to fill.
"Buck up, Cheesey, make it snappy,
"Mind you don't break dolly's cot."
And, still grunting, Father Christmas
Climbed down the last chimney pot.
Side by side they sat together,
Speeding homeward through the snow.
"Crumbs!" said Cheesecake, "Morning's dawning,
"And we've still a way to go."
"Don't keep moaning," said old Santa,
"Yes, I know you're tired out;
"We've a whole year to recover!
"Never mind about your gout!"
When at last they reached their igloo
Santa flopped down on his bed;
Cheesecake wasn't yet quite finished –
Rudolph still had to be fed.
When the chores were done, the doctor
Climbed in bed with Santa Claus;
Both felt they could sleep forever –
How the room shook with their snores!
Christmas morning, over breakfast,

Wearing funny paper hats,
Scoffing cornflakes, pulling crackers,
Giving each other playful pats,
Grinning broadly, pulling whiskers,
Both were now quite wide awake,
Then old Santa, turning serious,
Softly said: "Dr Cheesecake,
"You have been my faithful helper
"Over sixteen hundred years,
"Worked your fingers to the bone, and
"Shared my laughter, shared my tears.
"Helped me make the toys and presents,
"Helped me tie them up with string,
"Helped me take them round at Christmas –
"What a lot of joy you bring!
"But you're getting old, dear Cheesey,
"And I'm even older still,
"So I've done a bit of thinking
"(Pass the mince pies, if you will!)
"I've decided that this Christmas
"Is the last we'll do alone;
"When you get to our age, Cheesey,
"We can't do it on our own!"
Cheesecake heard all this in silence,
Then he gave a sudden laugh:
"But it's our *job*, Father Christmas –
"We can't take on extra staff!"
"Yes we can!" boomed dear old Santa,
"I arranged it yesterday!
"Advertised for one more helper!

"Our new elf starts right away!
"He'll prepare for next year's Christmas –
"Take the strain off us a bit!
"He'll be here soon after breakfast –
"You can issue him his kit!
"Come on, let's make this place tidy –
"Gobble up that last mince pie!
"Pop the dishes in the sink, now –
"You can wash, and I will dry!"

*circa 1980*

# PLAYSCHOOL[21]

I know a little girl called Amy Helen,
She went to playschool with Mrs Wellings[22];
When asked for her dinner money, she'd forgotten,
So Mrs Wellings smacked Amy's botton[23].

I know a little girl called Amy Helen,
She went to playschool with Mrs Wellings;
She gave her an apple, but it was rotten,
So Mrs Wellings smacked Amy's botton.

I know a little girl called Amy Helen,
She went to playschool with Mrs Wellings;
She did some writing and made a blot, an'
So Mrs Wellings smacked Amy's botton.

I know a little girl called Amy Helen,
She went to playschool with Mrs Wellings;
She went to the toilet, but missed the pot, an'
So Mrs Wellings smacked Amy's botton.

I know a little girl called Amy Helen,
She went to playschool with Mrs Wellings;
When offered a sweetie she ate the lot, an'
So Mrs Wellings smacked Amy's botton.

---

[21] A work of fiction. No children or animals were discommoded, or bottons smacked....

[22] Much loved headteacher at my daughter's first school.

[23] Polite word for "bottom", invented by my daughter – see page 84.

I know a little girl called Amy Helen,
She went to playschool with Mrs Wellings;
She took off her uniform 'cos she felt hot, an'
So Mrs Wellings smacked Amy's botton.

I know a little girl called Amy Helen,
She went to playschool with Mrs Wellings;
While sewing on a button she lost the cotton,
So Mrs Wellings smacked Amy's botton.

I know a little girl called Amy Helen,
She went to playschool with Mrs Wellings;
When told not to run she started to trot, an'
So Mrs Wellings smacked Amy's botton.

I know a little girl called Amy Helen,
She went to playschool with Mrs Wellings;
When told she was naughty she said "I'm not," an'
So Mrs Wellings smacked Amy's botton.

Etc[24].

*1980*

---

[24] Four hundred or so similar, and entirely predictable, stanzas deleted.

# THE SMELLY SONG[25]

You smell smelly,
Oh so smelly,
I can't tell 'ee how smelly you smell;
You're a stinker,
And, I think, a rotten ratbag as well.

You must be dotty,
Should say: "Potty!"
Then your grotty old nappy wouldn't hum,
And you wouldn't
Have to have Vaseline on your botton[26].

See that smelly mess in that nappy there?
                    *What nappy, where?*
What can that revolting mess be?
Is it your din-din?
Is it your supper?
Is it your breakfast?
Is it your lunch?
Is it your tea?

I'm not happy,
'Cos your nappy
Is all crappy and covered with ****;
I'm so angry
That I'm going to rub your nose in it.

---

[25] A song to be sung, preferably while changing a nappy, to a tune from a well-known musical – hopefully, the infant will eventually join in

[26] Polite word for "bottom". See page 84.

*La la la la la la la la la la!*

> *Have you seen my good friend Marcía –*
> *The smelliest girl in the place?*
> *She's hiding where no one can see her,*
> *But "guilty" is written all over her face.*
> *She's claiming that smell*
> *Was made by the dog, (la la la!)*
> *But she might as well*
> *Go straight to the bog!*

You smell smelly,
Oh so smelly,
I can't tell 'ee how smelly you smell;
You're a stinker,
And, I think, a rotten ratbag as well.

There's no telling,
Where this smelling,
And expelling, and plopping will end;
And I'm yelling
'Cos you've blocked up all the drains and u-bend.

See that smelly mess in that nappy there?
> *What nappy, where?*
How many more will there be?
Watch out there astern!
Makes my tummy churn!
Will you never learn?
When is Mummy's turn?
Why must it be me?
> *Why must it be me?*
> *Why must it be me?*
> *Why must it be me?*
> *Why must it be me?*

It's not funny!
You should runny
To the dunny when you need a poo;
Next time, Sonny,
I've a mind to flush you down the loo!

*La la la la la la la la la la!*

> *Have you seen my good friend Marcia –*
> *The prettiest girl on the block?*
> *She's hiding where no one can see her,*
> *But when you locate her prepare for a shock!*
> *She's claiming that smell*
> *Was made by the cat, (la la la!)*
> *But we know darn well*
> *That she has just ****!*

*Reprise*

You smell smelly,
Oh so smelly,
I can't tell 'ee how smelly you smell;
You're a stinker,
And, I think, a rotten ratbag as well.

Must be dotty,
Should say: "Potty!"
Then your grotty old nappy wouldn't hum,
And you wouldn't
Have to have Vaseline on your botton.

See that smelly mess in that nappy there?
What can that revolting mess be?
Is it your din-din?
Is it your breakfast?
Is it your supper?
Is it your lunch?
Is it your tea?

I'm not happy,
'Cos your nappy
Is all crappy and covered with ****;
I'm so angry
That I'm going to rub your nose in it.

1973

# OCCASIONAL WORMS

# A COVID ENCOUNTER

You snubbed me today!
(Not sure it was you –
You were wearing a mask;
I was wearing one, too…..)

*November 2020*

# THE DISAPPEARING TOMCAT[27]

My tomcat, Lucky, loved to fight!
He'd keep it up for half the night!
He once came home without an ear,
But still I found him very dear.
Though less of him came back to me
Than there had been before,
I filled him up with *Whiskas*, and
He loved me all the more.

One battle robbed him of an eye;
Another left him, high and dry,
Deficient by a leg, yet he
Had somehow hobbled home on three.
Though less of him came back to me
Than there had been before,
I filled him up with *Whiskas*, and
He loved me all the more.

Then someone told me what was wrong:
If he'd been neutered all along
Then fighting would've been no fun –
And so I went and had him done.
Though less of him came back to me
Than there had been before,
I filled him up with *Whiskas*, and
He loved me all the more.

---

[27] Another work of fiction. No children or animals were discommoded during the excretion of this doggerel.

Then all at once the fighting ceased,
But Lucky's luck, poor little beast,
Did not improve: while hunting snake,
I chopped his tail off by mistake.
Though less of him came back to me
Than there had been before,
I filled him up with *Whiskas*, and
He loved me all the more.

One day, poor Lucky fell quite ill;
I'd thought that it was just a chill,
So our vet's words filled me with dread:
"I've had to amputate his head!"
Though less of him came back to me
Than there had been before,
I filled him up with *Whiskas*, and
He loved me all the more.

One day, those naughty kids cajoled
Old Lucky into playing cricket;
One of them was out, clean bowled -
And they'd used Lucky for a wicket!
Though less of him came back to me
Than there had been before,
I filled him up with *Whiskas*, and
He loved me all the more.

So just Old Lucky's trunk was left,
And I was soon of that bereft.
He was sunning himself upon the grass.....
A motor mower chanced to pass.....
A thought occurred as I interred
Him 'neath the old hibiscus:
I should have drowned the litter, and
Saved all that sodding *Whiskas*!

*1982*

# EXERCISE

My wife thinks I am overweight
But feels it might be not too late
For me to shed a pound or two;
She even knows what I should do
To hold the extra inches in:
Cut out the beer, cut out the gin,
And do some press-ups on the floor.....
I must admit I'm not so sure.....

My wife believes I've gone to seed;
She puts it down to sloth and greed,
And too much sitting down, and worse,
Composing mediocre verse.....
My wife thinks I'm a tub of lard,
Though I think that's a trifle hard;
I feel I know what's for the best:
I reckon I need lots of rest.

My wife thinks I should get a bike,
And take a jog, or make a hike,
Or walk the dog, or run a mile:
No need for me to rest a while......
My wife wants me to join a gym,
To lift some weights or have a swim,
Or use the static row-machine.....
I must confess I'm not so keen.

My wife thinks I need exercise
Till blood is running out my eyes
And sweat is pouring down my back,
Until my tongue begins to crack,
And I am swooning in the heat,
And blisters bubble on my feet.....
But I'm not sure that this is true....
I think this all needs thinking through.

*June, 2015*

# POLYPHLOXIA

I think I might have leprosy:
It started with my nose,
Which came off in my handkerchief,
And when I checked my toes,
I found I just had five or six,
Though it was hard to tell…
I'd counted on my fingers, and
Found they were short as well.

I'm sure I must have leprosy:
To my acute dismay,
While I thought I was on the mend
My foot fell off today.
But when I went to A & E
To see if they could stop it,
The doctors didn't want to know –
They just told me to hop it.

*2021*

# ENOUGH'S ENOUGH

Joe, a *large* gin and tonic, if you'd be so kind,
And this time you can make it a treble!
There are moments like this when I need to unwind,
So I'll opt for a whopper, if you wouldn't mind,
For I'm starting to leave inhibition behind,
And beginning to whoop like a rebel......!

Now, come on, stop pretending to act like a tough,
I just *don't* find your attitude funny.....
And, believe me, I'm certainly calling your bluff
By insisting you serve me some more of this stuff –
Are you *really* suggesting that I've had enough?
Are you *really* refusing my money?

So, a large Devil's mouthwash, Joe, buddy divine,
Though you say I've already had seven;
Are you *sure* all these empties can really be mine?
*Look, I've no time to argue the toss, you fat swine,
'Cos I promised the Memsa'ib I'd be home by nine
And it's now nearly ten to eleven.*

OK, pour me a gargle, and cut out the chirps,
I can *always* make room for another....
Yes, I *know* that I'm choking on hiccups and burps,
But I'm not like the rest of these gin-sodden twerps,
I don't care if it's whisky or brandy – or turps –
Just stop trying to act like my mother.....

Right, decant me another one, Joe, if you will,
But you don't have to make it a double;
You are right that the extra one-sixth of a gill
Might be more than enough to upset the old bill,
Who could well be concealed at the foot of the hill,
And I'm not going looking for trouble.

Come on, Joe, be a sport, you just haven't a clue
How my Missus does *not* understand me.
But I always find sanctuary here, that is true,
So come on, be a gentleman – fix me a brew,
For I feel I can pour out my troubles to you –
You're the onliest pub that's not banned me.

Just the *teeniest* nightcap, Joe, don't be a bore.....
I don't need you to call me a taxi.....
Yes, you've already *said* I can't have any more,
And I *know* that I'm lying here, down on the floor,
But I tripped on your mat when I came through the door
And went a*** over t** on my jacksy.....

So just one for the road, Joe, and then you'll be free,
*You obtuse, oleaginous stinker... ...*
I am totally *sick* of your slick repartee,
No, I *don't* want a coffee, or nice cup of tea,
But if you'll share a stiff mother's ruin with me,
We'll *pretend* I'm a prim, social drinker.....

December 2019

# WEARINESS

Why does the sun on my back feel so chilly now?
Why must I button my vest to the neck?
Why do the good-looking dollybirds laugh at me?
How do they *know* I'm a physical wreck?

Why do I let the whole world trample over me?
Why are there problems I've never foreseen?
Why do I *never* win rock, paper, scissors, and
Who put the sand in my lube *Vaseline*?

Why are my entrechats not what they used to be?
Where is the offer I cannot refuse?
Who is that ugly old bloke in the shaving glass?
When did I switch from the rock to the blues?

Why does my football team lose every Saturday?
Why do my cricketers all score a duck?
Why, when I'm speaking, is nobody listening?
Why am I hurting, and who gives a toss?

Why is there nothing for me to look forward to?
Why are the good times so deep in the past?
When in my life have I ever won anything?
Why am I happy to always be last?

Why can't I write down the novels I feel in me?
Why are my operas never sublime?
Why do my paintings all smudge at the edges, and
Why do my attempts at epic poetry no longer even scan?
Or rhyme?

What have I done with the year since last Hogmanay?
What did I do with the previous ten?
When was the last time I did something useful? And
Was it as good as I thought it was then?

Why has my youthful ambition deserted me?
What would I do if it weren't for the booze?
Why have they stopped making blackcurrant *Spangles*, and
Why don't I **care** when the Albion lose?

What is the point of.....? Oh, bugger.....

*circa 1985*

# MY DACHSHUND

I took my dachshund walkies; he didn't want to go:
He bit me on the ankle, then bit me on the toe.
I said if he'd stop biting me he'd get a doggie treat;
He wagged his tail, and ate it – then bit me on both feet…

He bit me on the bottom, and then dragged me to the floor,
Then bit me on the elbow, and bit me four times more.
He bit me on the shoulder, and did I see him gloat
As he bit me on the pelvis, then bit me in the throat?

And as I lay there helpless he bit me on the thigh,
Then bit me on the cheekbone, and tried to bite my eye.
He simply wouldn't stop it; my arm was like a flute –
All black and blue and full of holes – the vicious little brute!

The blood was gushing wildly, but still he didn't rest:
He bit me in the armpit… He bit me on the chest…
He bit my Adam's apple, and bit me on the tum,
And bit me on the earlobe, and bit me on the thumb.

He bit me on the forehead, and even bit my hair;
In fact, when he was finished he had bitten everywhere.
And, as I lay there, bleeding, my strength was failing fast,
But then I had a stroke of luck: an ambulance drove past;

The medics stopped beside me to see what they could do,
And, while they were assessing me, my dachshund bit them too.
They put me on a stretcher, with very little wrangling;
My dachshund jumped and took a bite at bits of me still dangling.

They took me to the hospital and straight to A & E;
The doctor shook his head and said: "It's plain for all to see,
"Your body is a mass of holes; you've shed a lot of blood;
"It's pouring out from all your limbs and looks like *Noye's fludde*.

"You need a blood transfusion, which puts us in a mess:
"You're rhesus monkey negative and, what I must confess
"Is that we haven't any left – I thought that we had plenty,
"But when I checked our stock today I found that it was empty.

"I don't have many options, so where do I begin?
"We haven't any blood to spare – d'you mind if I use gin?"
"Oh no," I said, "please go ahead, I'm sure that gin's OK,
"But please avoid the cheaper stuff – do you have *Tanqueray*?"

"Oh yes," he said, "I've got all sorts – here, why not try a sip?"
And so I sank a large one, while he set up the drip.
And soon my veins were filling up with *Tanqueray* galore,
Till things were pretty much the same as they had been before.

When I was feeling well enough, and almost right as rain,
I hurried back to where I lived and soon was home again.
My dachshund barked when I went in; he watched me like a
        hawk…
"I think he's bored," my wife observed: "Please take him for a
        walk..."

So…..
I took my dachshund walkies….. He didn't want to go…..
He bit me on the ankle, then bit me on the toe.
Oh, lummee…..

*August 2019*

109

# TRANSISTERS

I'm moving up to Scotland soon,
As they've just passed a law
That says your gender needn't be
The one you had before.

So Scotland is the place for me,
As I am just the kind
Of crazy, mixed-up person who
Just can't make up his mind.

Sometimes a lad, sometimes a lass –
Alas! Sometimes I'm neither,
For I'm the kind of person who
Can't make up *her* mind, either!

But Scotland sounds the perfect place
For this recidivist:
No longer will I face the world,
My knickers in a twist…

I'll change my gender every day!
I'll do it on a whim!
When I'm fed up with being her
I'll just switch back to him!

And next time I am at the shops,
And looking for a loo,
I'll simply use the *Ladies* if
The *Gents* has got a queue!

I've written to the Minister,
With thanks for my new start,
For she's the kind of woman, who's
A man after my heart.

# THE PRICE OF FRIENDSHIP

There are some things cash just can't buy,
And friendship, on that list, is high;
It often comes at little cost –
Which doesn't mean that all is lost

If you've no bosom friend at all,
Forever at your beck and call,
(Though if you *do* have such a mate,
Who's always there for you – that's great!)

But if you're feeling sad and blue
And have no one to pull you through,
In ghastly times of strife and woe,
You're *not* completely lost! And so:

When all the world has let you down,
I'll be your friend, for half a crown;
And if you need some strong support,
For three and six you've got it bought.

You know you can depend on me
For everything, for four and three.
And if you need a little more
The works costs only six and four.

So come on, buddy, don't delay,
There's lots of easy ways to pay:
There's *Visa*, *Access*, cheque (uncrossed) -
I'll take them all (at extra cost).

So, drop that sad and sulky pout!
Rely on me to help you out!
I'm yours! For ever and a day!
(Unless you can't afford to pay...)

*circa 1973*

# EL DESILUSIONADO[28]

I always thought that you and me
Would hardly ever disagree;
That as we'd soldier side by side
Our thoughts would ever coincide.
I thought you'd always pull me through,
While I would do the same for you.
I trusted you implicitly,
So how could you do this to me?
I thought you'd never quit the fight,
I thought your thinking was all right;
That on the path of right, aligned,
We'd neither one be left behind.
You used to shun the leftie throng,
But now I see that I was wrong,
'Cos at the heart your faith was bad –
I'll never trust another Durham grad.
I must confess you had me fooled,
But what a dirty trick you pulled.
While I was in *Mein Kampf* immersed,
You went and wed on May the First.
It cut me deep, but best of all,
Upon this Commie festival,
You know who else will celebrate?

---

[28] Written for a friend's wedding anniversary. (It has been pointed out by some that, by coincidence, this one may be sung to the tune of *The Red Flag*.)

The *Lumpenproletariat*!
So now you see why I'm distraught,
As all my dreams have come to nought.
The blood and sweat and tears I've shed
Have slowly stained my black shirt red.
I wish that you could get your kicks
Without involving politics.
I wish you, too, adversary,
A happy anniversary.

*May, 1980*

# ENGLISH KINGS, 829-1066[29]

Egbert[30], Wulf[31], then Ett the Bald[32],
Bert[33], Red[34], Alfred[35], Ned the Auld[36],
Stan[37], Big Edmund[38], Eadred[39], Eadwy[40],
Edgar[41], Edward[42], Red Unready[43].
After Sven Forkbeard[44], the Dane,
Were we ready for Red again[45]?
Edmund Ironside[46], then Canute[47],

---

[29] A jingle to be used as an aide-mémoire in a history exam…
[30] Egbert 829-839
[31] Ethelwulf 839-856
[32] Ethelbald 856-860
[33] Ethelbert 860-865
[34] Ethelred 865-871
[35] Alfred the Great 871-879
[36] Edward the Elder 899-924
[37] Athelstan the Glorious 924-939
[38] Edmund the Magnificent 939-946
[39] Eadred 946-955
[40] Eadwig 955-959
[41] Edgar the Peaceable 959-975
[42] St Edward the Martyr 975-978
[43] Ethelred the Unready 978-1013 (first reign)
[44] Sven Forkbeard 1013-1014
[45] Ethelred the Unready 1014-1016 (second reign)
[46] Edmund April-November 1016
[47] Canute 1016-1035

Harold Harefoot[48], Hardecanute[49].
Confessor Edward[50] took some pastings,
But not like Harold Two[51] at Hastings.
Will[52] the Conqueror's next. Oh shoot!
(Edgar Atheling[53] doesn't fit!)

*circa 1982*

---

[48] Harold Harefoot 1045-1040

[49] Hardecanute 1040-1042

[50] St Edward the Confessor 1042-1066

[51] Harold II Jan-Oct 1066

[52] William I 1066-1087

[53] Edgar the Atheling Oct-Dec 1066, proclaimed but not crowned.

# DOGLESS[54]

I used to have a little dog,
I'd had him from a pup;
He really didn't like it if
Someone should pick him up.

He'd squeak and squirm, then whine and squeal,
And yap, then twist some more,
Until that someone took the hint
And put him on the floor.

Then he'd calm down, and all was well,
So I never forgot
That, though he was a lot of fun,
A lapdog he was not.

One day I took him to the vet,
So he could get his jabs,
To keep him free from whooping cough,
And foot and mouth, and crabs.

The vet, perhaps endeavouring
To soothe any alarms,
Picked up my dog, and stroked his head,
Cradling him in his arms.

---

[54] Another work of fiction. No children or animals were discommoded during the excretion of this doggerel.

"Put that dog down at once!" I cried –
The vet just shrugged: "OK…"
Then vanished somewhere out the back,
And took my dog away.

I never saw that dog again,
And don't know what to do.
They've sent me a bill for ninety quid –
Do you think I should sue?

*2024*

# NEVER POKE AN ODDBALL
# WITH A STICK

If you come across an oddball,
Do not poke him with a stick;
Though it's funny, he won't get it,
So it's certain you'll regret it,
And upset you, if you let it,
As he won't let you forget it –
More especially if you wet it,
(Or with needles you beset it,
Which would be a dirty trick…)

You may recognise an oddball
By the things he says and does.
If you're sure that they're not feigning,
Oddballs can be entertaining,
Though you'll frequently be straining
To recall your p.c. training,
Which you may find rather draining;
But you won't hear much complaining –
They can give you quite a buzz.

Don't expect to find all oddballs
Firmly locked up in a cage:
They're in any congregation,
And in every conurbation,
And in any occupation –
There are some who run the nation –
But don't yield to the temptation

That they may need provocation
Or you'll drive them in a rage.

So, however much you're tempted
Do not ever take the mick;
If you use a stick to bait him
It will only aggravate him,
And will certainly frustrate him,
And could well emasculate him,
If you clumsily castrate him,
So however much you hate him…
*Please…!* Don't poke me with a stick…

*circa 1980*

# JUST A THOUGHT...

I am a victim! It's so sad,
But this has to be said:
People like me are often far
Worse off alive than dead.
I'll not go into detail, but
You know the kind of thing:
Perhaps I'm persecuted as
My views are too left-wing.
Or it could be that there are those
Who think my thinking might
Be floundering in the middle ground,
Or shifting to the right.
So, either way, my fellow man
Has driven me to despair:
It's obvious we victims have
A heavy cross to bear.
Nobody loves me! That is clear,
But no one tells me why –
I can't work out the reason, and
It's better not to try.
Maybe I'm hated just because
I often choose to walk
On other people's flowerbeds...
And dribble when I talk...
Might folks object to what I smoke,
Or all my dirty habits,
Like using trees as public loos,
And biting heads off rabbits?
Or how I beat my wife and kids,
And kick my dog as well?
Or stroll about with nothing on,
And spit, and scratch, and smell?

And, since I never brush my teeth,
And never wash my hair,
But rinse my socks in public baths –
Is that why people stare?
Or don't they like it when I'm drunk,
And writhing in a stupor,
While singing loudly after dark,
And effing like a trooper?
The list is endless, but, alas,
Things won't improve, I fear,
Though, as I said, I really can't
Go into detail here.
But anyway, I've found a way
To crack this situation:
I think the government should now
Award me compensation.
No words can heal my hurt, of course,
So there'll be no forgiving;
But twenty million pounds up front
Might make my life worth living.
Don't think I'm being selfish here:
I'm not in this for me,
For everyone's a victim, too –
I'm sure you will agree –
So please don't think that I believe
I'm worse off than my brother:
We're all in some minority group
Of one sort or another.
So everyone, take my advice,
Get on to your MP,
And tell him from the heart that you're
A victim, just like me,

But twenty million smackeroos
Might mitigate your pain,
And, once you're paid, you'll disappear,
And not be seen again!
And when it has been recognised
That all our population
Is now a victim, I'll have solved
A problem for the nation:
No one will ever need to work,
As long as we draw breath:
We'll all have twenty million quid
To drink ourselves to death!

*2024*

# BIGOTS' CORNER[55]

I chanced to switch the telly on
And now I've seen it all!
Some women dressed as cricketers
Were playing bat and ball!

With stumps, and bails, and umpires,
And bats – *I kid you not!*
With boxes, creams, and caps, and pads –
I swear they had the lot!

I thought I'd stepped into a dream,
Or joined the funny farm –
I even noticed one fat lass
Was bowling overarm!

Despite the fact that this was Lord's,
Those *avant garde* females
Refused to focus on the game –
Third man was doing her nails!

One of the slips was sending texts,
Presumably to her mum;
Square leg was facing the wrong way,
(But what a lovely bum…)

---

[55] Where an attempt is made to dust off as many of the old, stereotypical clichés as possible, while satirising the views of any who may share the sentiments expressed.

The batsmen fiddled with their straps…
(As far as I could tell,
The fielding side all seemed, at times,
To fiddle with theirs as well…)

And neither batsman seemed to know
Which one of them should call,
As if their minds were somewhere else…
Perhaps – the shopping mall?

Deep backward point looked rather bored,
Though mid off looked *coquine*…
While long leg had the longest legs
That I have ever seen!

Wide silly point's attempt to catch
Looked silliest of all –
Leg gully must have glossed her lips,
And rubbed it on the ball!

The knowledge of the umpires
Was clearly miniscule:
I think they may have been confused
About the offside rule…

It seems those girlies, having fun,
Had glorified their game,
By calling it an *Ashes Test*!
Presumably, the name

Had come about because some gals,
A century ago,
Had gone and burnt a rolling pin
They'd rescued from the dough,

Then swept the ashes in a pile,
And hoovered them all up,
So they could use the sweeper bag,
As if it were a Cup,

And give it to the buxom lass
Who'd scored the winning run,
Then all rush home to ironing,
And making beds! What fun!

But, sad to say, as things progressed,
It seemed like counting sheep;
I struggled hard to stay awake,
But soon was fast asleep.....

The *Women's Ashes*, I'll confess,
Don't do a lot for me.....
It just means twenty-two poor blokes
Have gone without their tea.

*June 2023*

# EPITAPHS

# AN EX-WORDLER

Here lies a man who knew it all,
*WORDLE*'s unrivalled master;
But pride comes just before a fall,
Hubris before disaster.

His store of the five-letter word,
Unparalleled, and splendid,
Can now be, next to him, interred:
His streak has finally ended.

No group of five had stumped him yet,
He foresaw no succumbing;
But death's the one he didn't get:
He didn't see it coming.

*August 2023*

# HIC IACET OLD COL

Hic iacet old Col,
An unmemorable soul,
Who checked out when he ran out of money;
Now a thing of the past,
His demise was his last,
Sad, pathetic attempt to be funny.

*September 2021*

www.ingramcontent.com/pod-product-compliance
Lightning Source LLC
Chambersburg PA
CBHW032003040426
42448CB00006B/470